S.

WEIGHT AND BALANCE

Barbara Taylor

Photographs by Peter Millard

FRANKLIN WATTS
New York • London • Sydney • Toronto

Design: Janet Watson

Science consultant: Dr Bryson Gore

Primary science adviser: Lillian Wright

Series editor: Debbie Fox

The author and publisher would like to thank the following children for their participation in the photography of this book: Ozkan Aziz, Terry Cook, Corinne Crockford, Louise Fox, Thato Matebane, Daniel Seager, Stephen Wilkins and Rosemary Williams. We are also grateful to Julia Edwards and Evelyn Mildiner.

Thanks to Heron Educational Ltd for loaning equipment for use in the experiments and Lillywhites Ltd for the loan of sports equipment.

Illustrations: Linda Costello

Franklin Watts Inc.
387 Park Avenue South
New York
NY 10016

Library of Congress Cataloging-in-Publication Data
Taylor, Barbara, 1954-
     Weight and balance, Barbara Taylor.
        p. cm. – (Science starters)
     Summary: Discusses the concept of force and how the earth's gravity determines an object's weight. Introduces devices used to measure weight.
     ISBN 0-531-14082-2
     1. Gravitation — Juvenile literature. 2. Weights and measures — Juvenile literature. 3. Balance — Juvenile literature.
     [1. Gravitation. 2. Weights and measures. 3. Balance.] I. Title. II. Series.
     QC178.T238   1990
     530.8 — dc20   89-21504
                                            CIP AC

CONTENTS

This book is all about the balanced forces in structures and living things and how we measure weight. It is divided into five sections. Each has a different colored triangle at the corner of the page. Use these triangles to help you find the different sections.

These red triangles at the corner of the tinted panels show you where a step-by-step investigation starts.

BALANCE IN ACTION

Do you know why these people are leaning so far out to one side of the boat?

They are trying to balance the boat. If the people didn't lean over, the force of the wind would push the boat over. The weight of the people leaning in this position helps to stop this from happening.

Some everyday objects, such as this mug of toothbrushes, tip over easily. They are unstable. It needs only a small outside force in one direction to upset their balance. Cups for babies sometimes have a weight in the bottom to make them more stable and harder to tip over.

It takes a lot of force for a weightlifter to pull heavy weights up from the ground and balance them over his head. To keep the weights steady, the weightlifter has to push upward with a strong enough force to balance a force called gravity, which pulls everything on Earth down to the ground.

If something is not moving, then the forces acting on the object must be evenly balanced. These tree trunks are carefully balanced on top of each other. But if an elephant pushes hard enough, it can overcome the balanced forces and make the tree trunks roll down to the ground. This elephant is being taught how to lift and pull heavy tree trunks.

Have you ever taken part in a tug of war? If the people on one side pull harder than those on the other side, the rope will move. Once the rope is moving, if the other team pulls with even more force, the rope will move toward them more quickly.

Buildings have to be very carefully designed so that the forces in all the different parts of the structure are balanced. Steel wires are often set into concrete to help the building withstand the stretching forces that try to pull it apart. These stretching forces are known as tension.

A very strong outside force, like that of an earthquake, can upset the balanced forces inside buildings and make them fall down.

But if both teams pull with the same amount of force, the rope stays still. The forces are exactly balanced.

MAKE IT BALANCE

Next time you go to a park or a playground where there is a seesaw, try some experiments with balanced forces. If you sit on one end of a seesaw and two friends about your size sit on the other end, what happens?

With two children of equal size on each end, there is an equal amount of force pushing down on the seesaw. So it balances. To make the seesaw move up and down, the children need to add a little extra force by pushing their feet against the ground.

On this crane, can you see the heavy concrete blocks on the short arm? These are called counterweights. They balance the weight of the long arm and the load the crane is lifting. This stops the crane from falling over.

Look out for counterweights on cranes. They are easiest to see on the tower cranes that are used to build tall buildings. How big are the counterweights? Are they always in the same place?

Make a model seesaw.

1 Balance a ruler a little way above the ground on a fine point, such as a triangular piece of wood. The point at which the ruler balances is the fulcrum.

2 Place the same object on both ends of the ruler so that it still balances.

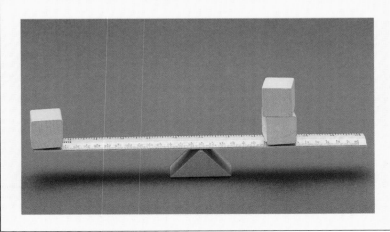

3 Now place two objects half-way between the fulcrum and one end of the ruler and place one object on the other end. The ruler should still balance.

This is because the two objects press down with twice the force at half the distance from the fulcrum.

Hold an apple in one hand and an orange in the other. Which feels heavier? Close your eyes to help you concentrate. Is your answer the same?

It is easier to find out the answer if you put the fruit on some scales. If they balance, the apple is just as heavy as the orange. In this case, the orange goes down slightly further, so the orange is heavier.

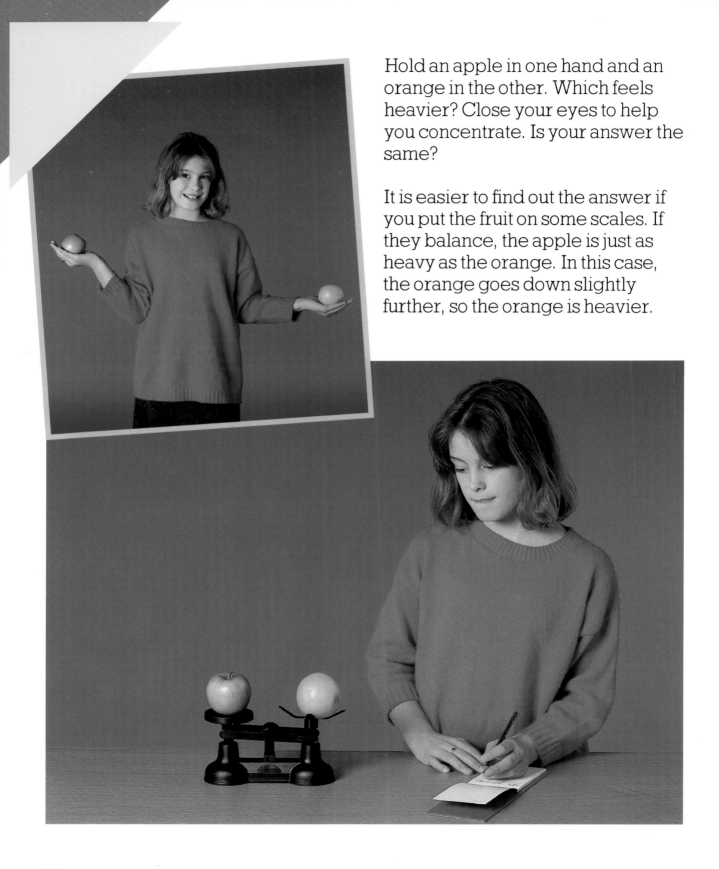

How many other fruits can you find that are heavier than apples?

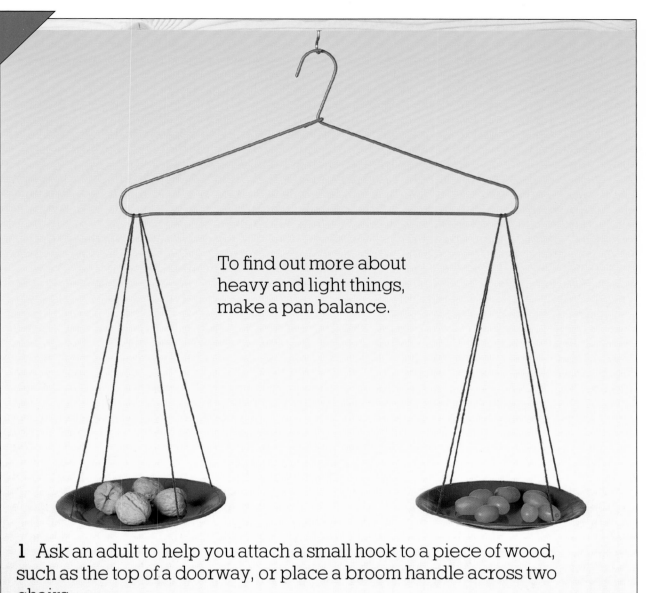

To find out more about
heavy and light things,
make a pan balance.

1 Ask an adult to help you attach a small hook to a piece of wood, such as the top of a doorway, or place a broom handle across two chairs.

2 Hang a coat hanger from the hook.

3 Find two paper plates and make four small holes around the edge of each plate.

4 Thread yarn or string through the holes, over the coat hanger and back through the holes again. Tie a knot in the yarn or string underneath the plate. If the wool or string slips, hold it in place with sticky tape. If the plates are not at the same level, make the yarn or string shorter or longer until the balance is about right.

5 Put small objects, such as grapes, nuts, beans, rice or paper clips onto the plates and see if you can make them balance.

MEASURING WEIGHT

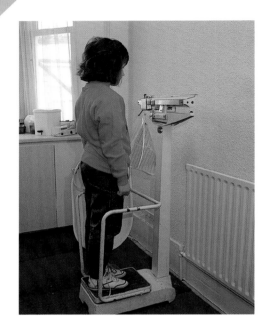

How heavy are you? When a doctor's scales balance, it tells the doctor how heavy you are in pounds. In everyday language, we call this our "weight," but to a scientist, this is not the correct word to use. Pounds measure the amount of "stuff" your body is made of and the correct word for this is "mass."

Weight is caused by the force of gravity pulling things down to the ground. It is measured in units called newtons. If the Earth had no gravity, objects on Earth would not weigh anything, but they would still have a certain mass. Inside scales, weight in newtons is converted into mass in pounds.

On the Moon, astronauts weigh only one sixth of what they weigh on Earth. The Moon is smaller than Earth and its gravitational pull is only one sixth of the pull of Earth's gravity. Astronauts can jump six times higher on the Moon, because there is less gravity pulling them down.

Don't forget that the mass of the astronauts is the same on the Moon as it is on Earth. The amount of "stuff" their bodies are made of doesn't change.

To measure mass (or "weight"), we sometimes balance objects against a known weight. This market trader puts pieces of metal that weigh a certain number of units (such as pounds) into one pan and adds vegetables to the other pan until both pans balance at the same level.

Most of the scales we use today, such as these kitchen scales, have a spring inside them. The spring stretches or squeezes together when we weigh something.

Try weighing things on some kitchen scales. After you put a bowl or other container on the scales, remember to set the scales to zero before you weigh anything.

COOKING

kidney beans

walnuts

lentils

rice

One of these
heaps of cooking
ingredients
weighs half as
much as the
others. Can you
guess which one it
is? (The answer is
on page 31.)

sugar

dried fruit

pasta

dried herbs

This man is using a weighing machine to make sure exactly the same amount of flour goes into each sack.

When you are cooking, it is a good idea to follow the recipe and carefully measure out the right amount of each ingredient. Otherwise the food may have a strange taste, for instance there may not be enough sugar or you may add too many spices or herbs.

Try measuring out different cooking ingredients yourself. Make sure they all weigh the same amount. You will find that some have a smaller volume than others. This means that the material they are made of is more tightly packed together.

WEIGHING MACHINES

If you pull a pair of suspenders, they will stretch a long way. But when you let go, they spring back to their original size and shape. Materials like these are called elastic materials. Rubber is elastic, so are hair and yarn.

You can use rubber bands to help you weigh things. When you hang an object, like a bag of oranges, on the end of the rubber band, it will stretch. When the object is removed, the rubber band springs back to its original length.

Find out how much the rubber band stretches under the pull of several different known weights, such as a one-pound bag of rice. Then you only have to measure the amount of stretch to work out the weight of the different objects.

Make a spring balance.

1 Ask an adult to help you make a spring by twisting a wire coat hanger around a broom handle.

2 Fix a pointer to one end.

3 Hang the other end on a hook.

4 Hang a container below the pointer.

5 Now you need to make a scale. Stick a piece of paper next to the spring. Put a known weight into the container. Draw a line on the paper to mark the level of the pointer. Add some heavier weights, one at a time, until you have a range of lines. Write the weight next to each line.

6 Use your spring balance to weigh other objects.

Spring balances are often used to weigh tiny babies to make sure they are gaining weight properly.

A weighing machine called a weighbridge is used to check the weight of trucks and other large vehicles. The weight of a truck is set by law, taking into account the safety of the vehicle and the amount of environmental damage it may cause.

Another type of weighing machine for heavy objects is called a steelyard. It was invented about 2000 years ago. These children are investigating a giant model of a steelyard. One child sits on a chair on the short arm. The other children pull a heavy counterweight along the long arm until the bar balances. The red pointer then shows how much the girl weighs.

Make a sensitive balance to weigh very light things.

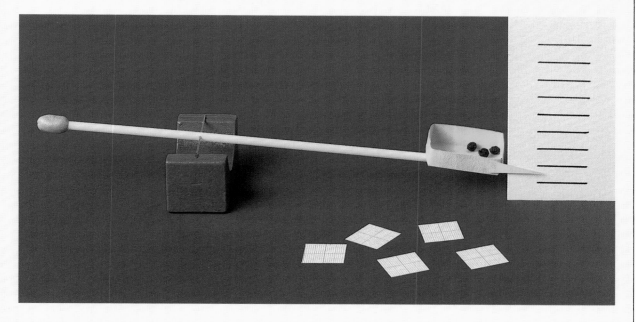

1 Push a needle through a straw about a third of the way along the straw. Balance the needle off the ground across two points.

2 Make a small paper tray and attach a pointer to one side of the tray. Stick the tray to one end of the straw.

3 Push modeling clay onto the other end of the straw until it balances.

4 Now you need to make a scale. Stand a piece of cardboard upright next to the pointer. Weigh a piece of graph paper on some scales. To find out the weight of each square, divide the weight of the paper by the number of squares. Then put one square at a time into your paper tray and mark the position of the pointer on the cardboard.

5 Use your sensitive balance to weigh objects like peppercorns, a pin, a leaf, a hair or even an ant.

Sensitive balances are used in scientific laboratories to measure weight very accurately.

FLOATING AND SINKING

Why do things float or sink? When an object is dropped into a liquid, such as water, it pushes some of the water out of the way. This is called displacement. To find out about displacement, carefully put a fruit, such as a melon, into a tank full of water. Make sure you catch any water that spills over the edge.

Then weigh the melon and the water (see page 13). They should weigh about the same. The melon floats because it displaces a weight of water equal to its own weight. If it displaced less water than its own weight, it would sink.

When you hang a brick from a spring balance, the force of gravity pulls it down and the air pushes up in the other direction. If you put the brick under water, it weighs less. This is because the water pushes up with a stronger force than air. The upward push of water is called buoyant force.

You can feel this force if you try and push a piece of polystyrene under the water in a bowl. It is hard to push the polystyrene because the water pushes back. When you let go of the polystyrene, the buoyant force pushes it back to the surface again.

OURSELVES AND ANIMALS

Your body is a complex balancing machine. Whenever you jump, run, skip or walk your brain automatically keeps the different parts of your body evenly balanced. You hardly notice this happening, unless you make a sudden or unusual movement and lose your balance.

How good are you at balancing? Can you balance on one leg on a skateboard? See if you can count to thirty before you lose your balance.

If you try to balance an apple on a book on top of your head, it is easier to use your arms to help you balance. Tightrope walkers use poles to help them balance. Try to balance a tennis racket in the palm of one hand.

Here are some balancing tricks to try with your friends.

Sit on a chair with your back touching the chair and fold your arms. Keep your feet flat on the floor. Now try and get up without leaning forward or moving your arms.

Now try standing next to a wall so that the whole of one side of your body is touching the wall. Make sure your foot, hip and face are all touching the wall. Can you lift your other foot and hold it in the air without falling over?

Turn the page to find out why these balancing tricks work.

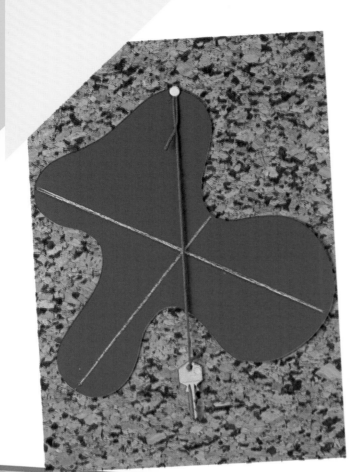

The pulling force of Earth's gravity on any object seems to be concentrated at one point. This is called its center of gravity or center of balance.

See if you can find the center of gravity of an irregular shape. Cut out the shape from a piece of cardboard and pin it to a bulletin board. Hang a piece of yarn or string with a weight on the end from the pin. The force of gravity will pull the yarn or string making it hang vertically.

Draw a line behind the yarn or string. Pin the shape at several different points and draw a line each time. The point at which the lines cross is the center of gravity of your shape.

Can you balance the shape from this point?

Your center of gravity is roughly in the middle of your chest. When you are standing upright, your brain tries to keep your center of gravity above your feet. This keeps your body balanced. In the balancing tricks on page 23, you can't keep your center of gravity over your feet without leaning forward on the chair or moving your other foot away from the wall.

When animals run, jump, climb or change direction quickly, they have to make careful adjustments to their balance so they don't fall over. Many animals have a special part of the body to help them in this difficult task... the tail.

A tail is usually long and heavy in order to balance the weight of the rest of the body. This parrot balances on its perch because it has a weight in the end of its tail. Without this weight, the parrot would fall over.

A tail is a kind of counterweight. Can you remember a machine that uses a counterweight? (Look back at page 9 if you get stuck.)

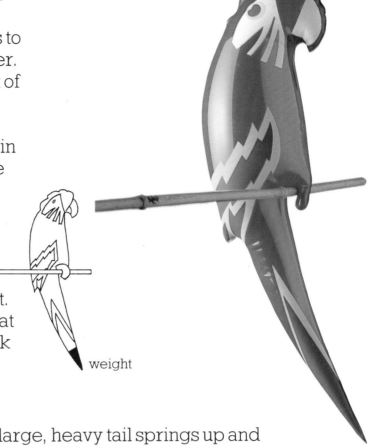

weight

When a kangaroo hops along, its large, heavy tail springs up and down to help it balance.

CARRYING LOADS

Have you ever built a house of cards? How many stories can you add before the house falls down? To make the cards balance, you have to think of the forces pushing and pulling the cards in different directions.

Scientists need to know as much as possible about forces to help them design buildings and bridges.

This wooden bridge in Cambridge, England, was originally built in 1749 without a single nail to hold the wood together. The pieces of wood are shaped and positioned to stay in place and carry the weight of people walking over the bridge. The strength of the bridge is due to the criss-cross arrangement of the wood and the arch shape, which carries the weight down to the ground on either side of the river.

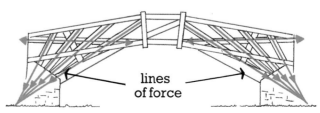

lines of force

Animal bodies are one of the most complex examples of balanced forces. Inside our own bodies, muscles constantly pull our bones in different directions in order to keep our bodies balanced.

It is easier for us to carry a load in a backpack on our backs than in a bag in one hand. The backpack allows us to keep our center of gravity over our feet and makes it easier to balance. It also spreads the weight out over the whole back.

When we use other animals, like camels, to carry heavy loads for us, we need to make sure the load is evenly balanced, especially if the load is a heavy one.

MORE THINGS TO DO

Your sense of balance

Your sense of balance depends partly on the movement of a fluid in your inner ear. As you move your head, this fluid moves too. It presses on some tiny hairs in your ear that convert the pressure into electrical signals (nerve impulses), which are sent to the brain. The brain acts on the information it receives and tries to make sure the body is balanced.

Put a pencil on the ground and walk around it four times. Now try and walk in a straight line. You will feel dizzy for a few moments and find it hard to keep your balance. This is because the fluid in your ears continues to swirl around. This confuses your brain and it tries to make you walk in a circle again, even though your eyes tell the brain you have stopped doing this. Once the fluid has stopped moving, you can balance properly again. Motion sickness happens when the balancing mechanism in your ears is upset in a similar way.

Recording weight

Weigh yourself at regular intervals during the day. Does your weight vary? If so, when are you heaviest? Weigh yourself after you have been playing sports or running fast. How does the exercise change your weight?

Ask your friends and family to tell you their weight. Draw a chart that compares the different weights. Are taller people heavier than shorter ones? Are older people heavier? Try to find out the correct weight for the different people on your chart.

How many newtons do you weigh?

Use some scales to find out your own mass in pounds. Every pound of mass is pulled down to Earth by a force of about 4.5 newtons. So if you multiply your mass in pounds by 4.5, this will give you your weight in newtons. For example, if your mass is 88 pounds, your weight is about 396 newtons.

Balancing water

Make a pivot by balancing a pencil on top of a block. Balance a ruler on top of the pivot. Find two identical egg cups and fill each one half full of water. Balance one egg cup on each end of the ruler. Adjust the water levels if the ruler does not balance evenly. Then put a finger carefully into one of the egg cups. Do not touch the sides or the bottom of the egg cup. What happens to the balance?

Your finger takes the place of some of the water and pushes it up the sides of the egg cup. This makes the egg cup weigh more, and so the balance tips down on that side.

Make a mobile

1 Draw and cut out several cardboard shapes.

2 Make a hole in one edge of each shape. Cut holes through both ends of a straw and pull some thread through the holes. Tie a shape to each piece of thread and knot the thread to keep the shapes in place.

3 Find the point where the straw hangs level (the balance point) and loop some more thread around the straw at this point. Pull the other end of the thread through a hole in one end of another straw.

4 Keep adding shapes and straws to your mobile until you have made several layers. Remember to begin the mobile from the bottom and work upward. Hang the mobile up where the air will push it around.

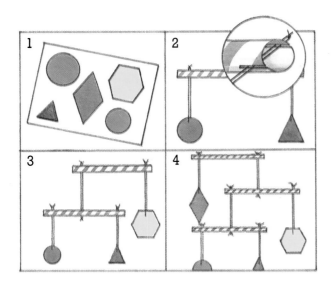

Make a balance

Some scientific balances use a ray of light reflected from a mirror to point to the scale. They are very sensitive. Make a simple version of this yourself to see how it works. Stick black paper or tape over a small mirror so only a thin strip of mirror shows. Use modeling clay to stick the mirror upright on one end of the ruler. Stick a small plastic lid on the other end of the ruler. Balance the ruler on a pivot, such as a triangular block. You may need to add or take away some modeling clay before the ruler will balance evenly.

Stand a scale near the ruler and shine a light onto the mirror. Make sure the light is reflected from the mirror to the scale. Use some known weights to make a scale (see page 16) and then use the balance to weigh small objects.

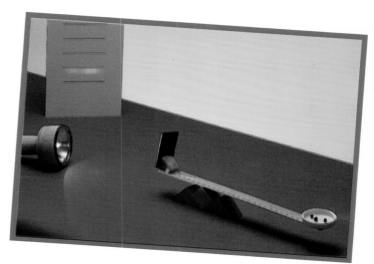

Balancing butterfly

Draw and cut out a butterfly shape. Stand a pencil upright in some modeling clay. Stick coins on the wing tips of the butterfly, as in the picture. Balance the butterfly on the pencil. Where is the balance point or center of gravity?

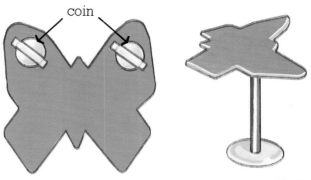

coin

29

DID YOU KNOW ?

▲ The heaviest animal alive today is the blue whale, which can weigh up to 200 tons. The huge weight of its body is supported by the buoyant force. Out of the water, it would be crushed by the weight of its own body. The heaviest land animal is the African elephant, which can weigh up to 10 tons – as much as 160 people. One pair of record-breaking elephant tusks weighed 260 pounds – as much as two people!

▲ The heaviest dinosaurs were sauropods such as *brachiosaurus*, which may have weighed 78 tons – as much as 8 large elephants. A land animal this size needed to eat about 882 pounds of plant material every day to stay alive.

▲ A tiny bird, the Vervain hummingbird of Jamaica weighs only 0.08 ounces. To stay alive, it has to eat half its body weight in food every day.

▲ A giant African snail can weigh up to 2.2 pounds. Some giant clams weigh almost 1,102 pounds – nearly as much as 8 people.

▲ There are lots of different sayings that use the words "weight" or "balance." Here are some examples: "to pull your weight"; "to weigh your words carefully"; "to throw your weight around"; "it's in the balance"; "to hold the balance of power"; "the balance of nature"; "to strike a balance"; "to settle the balance"; "the balance of payments"; "to follow a balanced diet."

▲ Every object, however small, has its own gravitational force and pulls other objects towards itself. This book is pulling you towards it, but the force is so weak you don't feel it.

▲ When you go up in an airplane, you weigh a little less because the pull of Earth's gravity gets less as you go further away from Earth.

▲ Each of the nine planets in the solar system has a different mass and therefore a different gravitational pull. For example, on Mars, things weigh only about half as much as they do on Earth.

▲ In a high jump, an athlete has to push upward against the pull of Earth's gravity. On the Moon, the best high-jumper could jump more than 46 feet, because the pull of the Moon's gravity is only one sixth as strong as the pull of Earth's gravity.

▲ The Metric system is based on international standards of length and mass. The international kilogram standard is a cylinder of the metals iridium and platinum, which weighs one kilogram. This piece of metal is kept in France and is maintained very carefully so that it will always weigh the same amount.

▲ The old British system of weights was based on numbers of grains of wheat or barley. One British pound was the weight of 7,000 grains of wheat or barley.

▲ The center of gravity of an object can be outside the object itself. The center of gravity of a doughnut is in the middle of the ring – in thin air.

▲ The heavy antlers of a reindeer or the large curving horns of a mountain sheep act as counterweights. The position of these heavy weights on the body helps the animal to keep its balance.

30

GLOSSARY

Axis
The point about which something turns.

Buoyant force
The upward force equal to the amount of displaced fluid.

Center of gravity
The place where the entire weight of an object appears to be concentrated. It is also called the center of balance.

Counterweight
A weight used to balance another weight that is pulling an object in an opposite direction.

Displacement
The amount of water or another liquid pushed out of the way by a floating object. A floating object weighs the same as the liquid it displaces.

Elastic material
A material that returns to its original shape after a stretching force is removed.

Gravity
The force of attraction between any two objects that have mass. The strongest gravitational pull on you comes from Earth.

Mass
The amount of matter, or "stuff," a body contains. It is measured in pounds and is often incorrectly called "weight."

Newtons
The unit used to measure force. One newton is the force needed to accelerate an object with a mass of 2.2046 pounds by 3.280 feet per second every second.

Spring balance
A weighing machine in which the weighing is carried out by the stretching or pressing together of a spring.

Stable object
One that is fixed firmly in position, so it cannot easily be tipped or knocked over.

Steelyard
A balance consisting of a beam with one long arm and one short arm. The object to be weighed is hung on the short arm and a sliding weight is moved along the long arm until the beam balances.

Tension
A strain produced by pulling or stretching.

Weighbridge
Machine for weighing vehicles, heavy machinery or railroad engines. A weighbridge has a flat plate, either level with the ground or just above it, so that heavy machines can be pushed, rolled or driven onto it. It consists of a number of different levers arranged so that only a small weight is needed to balance the heavy weight loaded onto the plate.

Weight
The force exerted on objects by the pull of gravity. It is measured in newtons. Things have weight because gravity pulls them down to the ground. The greater the pull of gravity on an object, the more it weighs.

Answer to question on page 14: dried herbs.

INDEX

Additional photographs:
Alan Cork 6t, 27b; Eye Ubiquitous
12t, 18t; David Exton/Trustees of
the Science Museum (LP129) 18b;
Chris Fairclough 15t, 17br;
Hutchison Library/Chris
Oldroyd 13t; Hutchison
Library/Jorge Vertiz 7t; Hutchison
Library/J G Fuller 26b; courtesy of
Mettler Instruments Ltd 19tr;
Peter Millard 9t; courtesy of NASA
12b; Survival Anglia/Des and Jen
Bartlett 25b; ZEFA 4.
Picture researcher:
Sarah Ridley